EDITOR Conor Sweetman
EDITOR IN CHIEF Russell Moore
CREATIVE DIRECTOR Sarah Gordon

DESIGNER Alecia Sharp
ILLUSTRATIONS BY Sandra Rilova
PRODUCTION DESIGN BY Rick Szuecs

COPY EDITING BY
Raicheal Fulle
Sara Kyoungah White

A TIME FOR
WONDER

THE DAYS OF ADVENT THROUGH
THE EYES OF WORSHIP

CONTENTS

WORDS FROM THE EDITOR

BY CONOR SWEETMAN

The Christmas season might seem like an odd time to turn to Ecclesiastes in your Bible. As December dawns, there's no time to ponder the ephemerality of life—the house needs cleaning! The cookies need baking! The presents need wrapping! The family needs to be entertained! Or maybe the season that feels bereft of spare time is exactly the moment to ponder the fleeting nature of our lives.

We often engage a wide spectrum of experience during this unique season. Ecclesiastes bears testimony to the reality that there is a specific time for everything—for planting and sowing; for crying and laughing; for lamentation and celebration. Wherever the Christmas season finds you this year, you can take heart in the fact that God orders reality according to seasons and rhythms that are sometimes dark and sometimes light; sometimes heavy and sometimes full of levity.

In this Advent devotional from Christianity Today, we move through the cycle of morning, afternoon, and evening, each with its own tone and specific reality to press into. As we move through the weeks of Advent, this devotional guides us along a journey through times of renewal, trial, revelation, and ultimately to a time of wonder at the great gift that we have at Christmas: Christ's incarnation on Earth, his taking on flesh for the sake of love and our salvation. Dive in, find the time to witness the days of Advent through the eyes of wonder, and join as we worship together. ■

CONTRIBUTORS

Meet the team of writers whose dedication and passion have filled the pages of this Advent Devotional with stories of faith, hope, and love. We hope their commitment to excellence and their exploration of the depths of Christian life will offer this devotional as a beacon of light during the Christmas season.

JULIA BARTEL

Julia Bartel is a recent graduate of the University of St Andrews' Institute for Theology, Imagination, and the Arts. She lives in Scotland.

JONATHAN CHAN

Jonathan Chan is a writer and editor. Born in New York, he was raised in Singapore and educated at Cambridge and Yale.

ISAAC GAY

Isaac Gay is an artist, worship leader, and writer at the crossroads of creativity, spirituality, and contemporary thought.

ALICIA HAMILTON

Alicia Hamilton authors Bible studies and disciples college students in New Hampshire.

AARON CLINE HANBURY

Aaron Cline Hanbury is a writer and editor.

CHRISTINA GONZALEZ HO

Christina Ho is the author of the audio series "The Last Two Years" and the cofounder of Estuaries.

JASMINE JONES

Jasmine Jones is a mentor and connector, passionate about empowering others to boldly live out their faith through her online community, The Purpose Corner.

LILY JOURNEY

Lily Journey is a non-profit professional, poetry enthusiast, event creative, and writer.

RYAN KEATING

Ryan Keating is a writer, teacher, and pastor on the island of Cyprus. His poetry can be found in publications such as *Ekstasis* and *Fare Forward*.

VIJAY KRISHNAN

Vijay Krishnan is the lead pastor at The Well in the Greater Toronto Area. Vijay, Jennifer and their 3 boys love being a part of what God is doing through the local church.

GABRIELLE MCCULLOUGH

Gabrielle McCullough is an evangelist and Bible teacher currently in Waco, Texas, eager about reaching all people with the gospel of Jesus Christ.

ANDREW MENKIS

Andrew Menkis is a theology teacher, with his poetry and prose published in *Modern Reformation*, *Ekstasis*, *The Gospel Coalition*, and *Core Christianity*.

MORGAN MITCHELL

Morgan Mitchell serves as a pastor in San Diego, specializing in church small groups, discipleship, and preaching.

COURTNEY MOODY

Courtney Moody is a ballet dancer, writer, and poet of faith. Her publications include *Ekstasis* and *The Way Back to Ourselves* literary journal.

RICH PEREZ

Rich Perez served as a pastor and public speaker for 20 years. Today, he is a filmmaker, crafting narratives for brands and organizations.

KIMBERLY PHINNEY

Kimberly Phinney is a writer and professor. She is founder of the literary community www.TheWayBack2Ourselves.com and has been published in *Ekstasis*.

CALEB SAENZ

Caleb Saenz is lead pastor
of The Garden, a church
planted in San Antonio in 2023.

KEN SHIGEMATSU

Ken Shigematsu is the senior pastor
of Tenth Church in Vancouver.
He's the author of bestsellers *God in My
Everything* and *Survival Guide for the Soul*.

ALYSSA STADTLANDER

Alyssa Stadtlander is a writer and actress
based in Boise, Idaho. Her work
is published in *Ekstasis*, *Mudfish
Magazine*, *Fathom*, and others.

KAREN STILLER

Karen Stiller is author of
Holiness Here, *The Minister's Wife*,
and other books about the church.

GEORGE SWEETMAN

George Sweetman has served
as the dean of student life at
Tyndale University in Toronto
for the past 25 years.

W 1

A TIME FOR

RENEWAL

"Awake, my soul!
Awake, harp and lyre!
I will awaken the dawn."

PSALM 57:8

THE EVENT HORIZON OF ADVENT

The Christmas season shows us
our redeemed past and hopeful future.

BY ANDREW MENKIS

I ONCE HEARD SOMEONE CLAIM that if you could enter a black hole and reach the event horizon, you would see into the past and future simultaneously. My attempts to wrap my head around this have not yet been successful. I'm no physicist, but I do understand what it is like to stare at my past or to try to see into my future.

Typically, this causes problems. Looking to the past often leads to regret, shame, or depression about what has happened and cannot be changed. Looking to the future often leads to worry, fear, or anxiety about what may happen. The reason for this, I think, is that my gaze is focused solely on myself. In contrast, Christ calls us out of ourselves to look to him. During the Advent season we are invited to look to the past at what Christ has done, even as we look to the future hope of what he will do when he comes again.

David had his eyes set upon Christ when he composed Psalm 110. In the opening lines, God speaks to someone that David calls, "my lord." In other words, God is talking to King David's king. This King of Kings is our Savior, Jesus Christ (Acts 2:34–36). The psalm paints a portrait of Christ as victor over God's enemies, ruler of the nations, powerful, vibrant, and just. As if this picture wasn't magnificent enough, the psalm adds another layer to the image: Christ is also a priest after the order of Melchizedek. The author of Hebrews explains why this is significant: "[Melchizedek is] without father or mother, without genealogy, without beginning of days or end of life, resembling the Son of God, he remains a priest forever" (Heb. 7:3). Christ is an eternal priest, unlike the Levitical priests of the Old Testament, a perfect and continuous mediator, intercessor, and advocate between God and his people.

In this poem, David invites us to focus our thoughts, our affections, and our desires on a vision of the priest-king Jesus Christ. As we look into the past and behold the birth, life, suffering, crucifixion, resurrection, and ascension of Christ we are drawn out of our regret, shame, and depression. Christ is king; he has the power to ensure there is nothing that has happened to us, or by us, that God will not use for good (Rom. 8:28). Christ is our priest; all our shame and guilt has been dealt with on the cross. More than that, Christ has conquered death and the Holy Spirit who brought Christ to life dwells in us, giving us new life and hope for the future. Our worries, our fears, and our anxieties are put into proper perspective when we look to Christ and remember that just as he came once, he will come again to destroy evil, uphold justice, and save his people.

For a psalm so full of violent imagery—enemies made into a footstool, shattered kings, corpses filling the nations—David ends on a surprisingly calm note. In the midst of judging the nations the priest-king stops to take a break. The final portrait David paints for us is of Christ, pausing to take a drink of cool, refreshing water from a brook, then lifting up his head (v. 7). His pause indicates that the end of all things is not yet upon us. We stand in our present moment—the event horizon, if you will—between the first and second coming of Christ. Rather than obsessively staring at our own past or future, through this psalm, Christ invites us to look at him to find forgiveness, identity, peace, security, and hope in what he has done for us in the past, and in what he will do when he returns in the future to establish his reign as priest and king, once and for all. ∎

REFLECT

David invites us to focus our thoughts and desires on Christ. How can you practically shift your focus from yourself to Christ during this Advent season?

Reflect on your own tendency to dwell on the past or worry about the future. How does dwelling in the words of Psalm 110 reshape your perspective?

PAVING THE WAY FOR GOD'S PERFECT PLAN

John the Baptist reveals
the call of preparation.

BY JASMINE JONES

THERE'S SOMETHING about the idea of starting from zero that makes me want to run and hide. As a recovering perfectionist, I like a beautifully constructed plan that articulates all the ins and outs of how things are supposed to go. The thought of being the one to "pave the way" without a guide or rule book is a daunting prospect for me. Have you ever been there? Maybe you've been the one who was called to be the "first" in your family. The first to graduate from college; the first to move outside of your hometown; the first to become a Christian.

This is the position John the Baptist found himself in before he was even born. In Luke 1:17, we find the angel of the Lord proclaiming the pioneer that John would be: "And he will go on before the Lord, in the spirit and power of Elijah, to turn the hearts of the parents to their children and the disobedient to the wisdom of the righteous—to make ready a people prepared for the Lord." John was left with the honorable, and I'm sure unnerving, task of preparing people for Jesus, the promised Messiah. How's that for paving the way?

And while I know that God equipped John with everything he needed before he was put on this earth, I can't help but think about the weight and real human emotions that John might have felt and been burdened by. Was he afraid of making a wrong decision? Was he overwhelmed by the idea of authentically articulating who Jesus is? I can't imagine starting at square one with no books on evangelism, no sinner's prayer or sermon illustrations.

It's easy for impostor syndrome to kick in when we look at "paving the way" through the lens of our own abilities. But the beautiful lesson we learn from the life of John the Baptist is that paving the way has nothing to do with our abilities, and everything to do with our availability to God's call. Being an available vessel grants us the privilege of being in constant collaboration with the Spirit at work within us. And when we are operating from that place of collaboration, there's no task or call too big for God to accomplish.

He used an old, unlikely couple and their baby as the vessel to spread the good news about the coming of the Savior of the world. Though it will inevitably look different in our own lives, it can be powerful to contemplate what God is inviting us personally to be a vessel for through the Advent season and beyond. It is clear through the lineage of Jesus that God delights in working through our imperfect, unlikely stories to shine his light and love . . . even if that means you're one of the "firsts" in your sphere of influence to do so. As Christmas dawns and we consider the life of John the Baptist, paving the way for Jesus and his world-changing work, we can consider the invitation that God has bestowed upon our own lives, and whether we will accept it. It may be that there is a host of people you're paving the way for. ■

REFLECT

Consider John the Baptist's role in preparing the way for Jesus. How does his example inspire you to be open and responsive to the ways God might use you in your own community?

Consider in what specific areas of your life God might be inviting you to "pave the way" for others?

THE SONG OF MARY STILL ECHOES TODAY

How the Magnificat speaks
to God's care for the lowly.

BY RICH PEREZ

THE CHRISTMAS STORY is full of surprising celebration, even in the midst of challenging circumstances. Spending time with Mary's *Magnificat* brings a unique event to mind: Imagine a small team from Nicaragua reaching the Little League World Series, only for most parents to be unable to attend due to immigration hurdles. Yet, across six states, the Nicaraguan American community rallied, traveling to the games and offering a chorus of support in place of absent parents. This heartwarming display of solidarity that occurred in the summer of 2022 captures for me the essence of Mary's response to God's invitation in Luke 1.

Advent, a season of anticipation for Jesus' arrival, also compels us to examine the backdrop: a world of darkness, poverty, and desperation. Mary and Joseph find themselves on the run, seeking refuge for the birth of their child. Yet, amid the shadows, light arrives and beckons us to embrace its warmth.

The core message? God's promises often blossom in the most improbable circumstances. Luke 1 paints a vivid picture: The angel Gabriel announces Mary's pregnancy, and instead of succumbing to fear, Mary bursts into song. Her song isn't a plea, but a declaration of faith, a melody brimming with comfort for us.

Mary's song, particularly verse 48, reveals the cornerstone of her faith: "He has been mindful of the humble state of his servant." The phrase "humble state" signifies poverty, insignificance, and captivity. Mary recognizes her reality as a marginalized woman

23

in a society that often disregarded women and ostracized the poor.

This scene plays out in the marginalized communities today—immigrants, people of color, those struggling on the fringes. Yet, Mary's song transcends circumstance. It whispers hope, reminding us that God isn't a distant god, but one who sees us right where we are.

Mary's song echoes another unlikely heroine–Hannah, an elderly, barren woman ostracized for her childlessness. Yet, God remembered her (1 Sam. 1:19). Hannah's song, defying the social norms of her time, finds a new voice in Mary. This connection isn't accidental. Luke draws the connection between these remarkable women, reminding us that God's favor often rests on those deemed insignificant.

Think of unlikely mothers throughout history—Sarah, Rebekah, Rachel—who birthed pivotal figures in God's plan. God chooses the seemingly barren, the overlooked, to showcase his power. His promises flourish in the soil of impossibility.

Mary concludes her *Magnificat* with a powerful declaration: "He has helped his servant Israel, remembering his mercy to Abraham and his descendants forever" (Luke 1:54–55, CSB). This is a testament to God's unwavering faithfulness. He keeps his promises, fulfilling the prophecy whispered in Genesis 3:15 and the covenant established with Abraham in Genesis 12:3.

The celebration of Jesus' birth isn't just about God's faithfulness, it's about the fulfillment of our deepest yearning—a Savior who redeems us.

Mary's encounter with God compels us to action. True gospel enjoyment means solidarity with the margins from which it came. Jesus didn't just offer salvation; he walked with the ostracized, the hurting.

In moments of doubt, confusion, or despair, the most potent act of faith is to stand with someone else, witnessing the birth of their promise. Just as Mary journeyed to support Elizabeth, we are called to create a community of support, a chorus of encouragement for those on their own difficult journeys. May we, like Mary, find solace in God's presence. May we seek him in the faces of loved ones and strangers alike. May our hearts burn with the warmth of his love, a beacon of hope in a world yearning for light. ■

REFLECT

In what ways can Mary's song shape your perspective on God's character and care for all people, regardless of their societal status or circumstances?

Considering Mary's humility and trust in God's plan, how can you cultivate a deeper sense of surrender and openness to God's leading in your daily decisions?

THE UNEXPECTED FRUIT OF BARRENNESS

How the kingdom of God
delights in grand reversals.

BY ALICIA HAMILTON

I SAT ON THE COUCH AND WEPT, still dressed in stiff business casual. I had returned home from the classroom with the realization like a cold stone in my gut—I was not healthy enough to be a teacher. I could not finish my master's program. I could not spend the hours or energy required to do this one thing I thought God had been leading me toward my whole life. This garden I planted and tended since my childhood, just now springing up, was to die.

So, I gave it up. There was nothing to be done but pray that God would do something beautiful in the uprootedness of it all. I stood in the middle of dead dreams, unsure how—or what—to replant.

While in vastly different times and with different implications, I find a resonance in the story of Jesus' lineage and the way Elizabeth made her home in the wreckage of her uprooted dream. Her pain of a lost dream was compounded by the dishonor that barrenness brought in the ancient Near East. But in a moment, God reversed her story. "'The Lord has done this for me," she proclaimed. "In these days he has shown his favor and taken away my disgrace among the people'" (Luke 1:25). Here was hope, growing soft and green in the darkness of the soil, as surprising as spring. God specializes in epic reversals. Elizabeth would bear not just any son in her old age—she was carrying the child who would prepare the way for the Messiah.

I was still on that couch with crumpled tissues clenched in trembling hands when a wise man, now my husband, helped me sort out what was still growing in the garden: those seeds planted by the hand of God that I had missed. Years later, I'm harvesting different fruit than I thought I would—but it's better fruit. I consider this my own mini-reversal. God took a dream I thought had been rendered useless and flipped it into a reality of teaching through writing and discipleship, things that fit the contours of my heart better than a classroom could. I've made my home in this garden, and I can't imagine it any other way.

God's reversals fill the pages of Scripture. Consider the birth of Isaac to an elderly and once seemingly barren Abram and Sarai, Joseph's rise from slave to ruler, or the way Haman's plan to destroy the Jews was foiled by two Jews God lifted to positions of power in their place of exile. These stories speak to the way God delights in flipping situations upside down, bringing salvation in the most surprising ways.

All of these foreshadow the most surprising reversal of all. God was born as a baby to usher in the upside-down kingdom of heaven where the last are first. He defeated death and rose from his garden grave as the firstborn in the resurrection, purchasing our eternal life.

This ultimate reversal that flipped the principalities and powers upside down is what Elizabeth's reversal first points to. Having a child meant that she would no longer be called barren, undoing her earthly shame. But the baby Mary carried would undo Elizabeth's eternal shame. When Mary's greeting reached Elizabeth's ears, "the baby leaped inside her, and Elizabeth was filled with the Holy Spirit. Then she exclaimed with a loud cry, "Blessed are you among women, and your child will be blessed!" (Luke 1:41-42, CSB). Elizabeth's awe of God swelled as the Savior of the world, still in a womb, came through her door in the swollen belly of a virgin. The baby in Elizabeth's womb leaped, like hope springing up, because Mary's baby had arrived to save us.

This God is leading us home to the new heaven and earth, a beautiful garden city where death is no more. And until then, he is planting new life in you and me. Our God gives us something better than our earthly dreams. He gives us himself. ■

REFLECT

Reflect on a time in your life when a dream or plan did not come to fruition as you had hoped. How did you see God at work in that situation?

Consider the theme of God's grand reversals in Scripture and in your life. How do stories like Elizabeth's encourage you to trust in God's ability to bring about surprising and redemptive outcomes in seemingly hopeless situations?

THE SURPRISING ARRIVAL OF A SERVANT

Jesus' introduction of justice
through gentleness.

BY JONATHAN CHAN

MAN OF SORROWS, *lamb led to the slaughter.* At the time of their recording in Isaiah 53, there was every possibility that these monikers would remain purely abstract. The Israel addressed in Isaiah is to face judgment, exile, and restoration under Assyrian captivity and Babylonian invasion. To a people under duress, Isaiah's prophecies helped endow a messianic imagination and a vision of a salvific figure.

But the first suggestion that this figure would not take on the form of a military revolutionary, as some might have hoped, lies in the word *servant*, from the Hebrew word *ebed*, used throughout Scripture to variously connote a slave, a vassal king, a subject, and a tributary nation. The word foretells a chosen servant who receives the delight of the Lord and the Spirit, and who brings long-awaited justice to the nations.

Meekness, humility, and modesty characterize Christ from the start, who came into this world as flesh and blood, as an infant in full vulnerability. He is close to the hearts of all those who suffer, including those who face the physical corrosion and psychological turmoil of poverty, disaster, and war. Christ was born into a world that had sought to destroy his infant flesh; the slaughter of the Holy Innocents under Herod's heinous regime is evidence enough of this earthly brokenness. It is, as the poet Czesław Miłosz describes in his poem "Theodicy," a world that "lies in iniquity," where "there is pain, and the undeserved torture of creatures." It is a world to which the servant described by Isaiah must bring justice.

Yet this justice is to come through an exquisite tenderness, a strength that lies precisely in gentleness. A reed that is bruised is so frail as to snap at the slightest touch, yet this servant shall not break it. A wick that burns faintly is close to being snuffed, yet this servant shall fan it back into flame. It is Christ who sees possibility and hope for the bruised, for the weary, for the exhausted.

Theologian Eugene Peterson once explained in *Eat This Book* that a metaphor is "a word that bears a meaning beyond its naming function; the 'beyond' extends and brightens our comprehension rather than confusing it." The metaphors of the reed and the wick help to illuminate an understanding of human difficulty; the actions taken by the servant illustrate how Christ tends to the lowly. It is, as Dane Ortlund describes in *Gentle and Lowly*, Christ's most natural instinct to move toward sin and suffering.

This is the Messiah for whom the world waited amid the silence of God—the one we commemorate in the season of Advent, in which each day is suffused with the dark mystery of anticipation.

At the heart of faith is a contradiction: a Savior born to die, an infant whose being prefaces a demise by the cruelest of tortures. Even under such indescribable physical, emotional, and mental duress, this servant will become neither faint nor discouraged. Justice will roll over the earth, not just from the jagged deserts familiar to the lands of ancient Jerusalem but beyond, to the distant coastlands that reach the waters.

It is a victory, a realization of justice that is achieved by servanthood, an obedience to the point of death (Phil. 2:8). It is an example of William Langland's *Pacientes vincunt*—the patient are victorious, or perhaps, those who suffer shall win. Or as the imagined voice of Christ cries out in Shūsaku Endō's novel *Silence*, "It was to be trampled on by men that I was born into this world. It was to share men's pain that I carried my cross."

Christ comes into the world as an infant, growing in the obedience and servanthood for which he has been called. Advent brings this swell of anticipation—a cradling of hope—for the arrival of the Savior, by whom justice will be established on earth through the humility of servanthood. ∎

REFLECT

Consider the metaphors of the bruised reed and the faintly burning wick. How can you see hope and potential in the weary and exhausted areas of your life?

Consider the paradox of a Savior born to die; a servant who achieves victory through suffering. How does this affect your understanding of what it means to live a life of faith and servanthood?

Recall and reflect on the many stories of renewal from this week. Allow them to prepare your heart for the Advent season.

Whose story did you most resonate with?

DAY 1 King David

DAY 2 John the Baptist

DAY 3 Mary

DAY 4 Elizabeth

DAY 5 Isaiah

Why?

How do the stories of this week allow you to see God's work of renewal both in your own life and through the grand narrative of Scripture?

W 2

A TIME FOR

TRIALS

"From the ends of the earth I call to
you, I call as my heart grows faint;
lead me to the rock that is higher than I."

PSALM 61:1-2

AFTER DISASTER, GOD DRAWS NEAR

How Jeremiah's prophecy
points to Advent's promise.

BY AARON CLINE HANBURY

THE PROPHET JEREMIAH writes from a social, political, and spiritual landscape cramped and dark, like falling into a pit, humid and heavy with the weight of regret. His words, the message from God, match the tone. Read any part of Jeremiah's prophecy and you'll see the theme: the failure of God's people. They couldn't keep their part of the covenant God made with them, and the young prophet delivers God's response with unflinching force. Right in the beginning, Jeremiah's earliest vision establishes what will follow: "From the north disaster will be poured out on all who live in the land" (Jer. 1:14).

Like Moses before him, Jeremiah initially protests the work God has called him to do, proposing his age as a disqualifier (Jer. 1:6). By traditional accounts, Jeremiah heard the call from God around 627 B.C., which makes him something like 20 years old when the book opens. For 40 years, he continues warning of a disaster from the north.

Not unlike the time of the judges, God's people are once again caught in a vicious, self-induced spiral of breaking their commitments to God and seeking vindication and consolation anywhere and everywhere else. Jeremiah delivers news of God's wrath, and he prophesies about the ways God will respond to the people's unfaithfulness.

The disaster arrives in 587 B.C. as Babylon destroys Jerusalem, bringing swift destruction to what had been eroding for centuries. Like a flood, the prophesied pouring-out wipes out God's dwelling place in the land of Israel—an undoing of creation.

You could fairly assume that for a person like Jeremiah—an Israelite from Benjamin's tribe—these were times more dire than what we see in Judges. That was before David, before the temple. With the breaking of Jerusalem, David's kingdom washed away in a flood of Babylonian destruction. Jeremiah occupies this undone space.

Jeremiah hears from God not to take a wife or have children. At this point in history and within this Israelite culture, you'll find no category for a single, childless man. One Old Testament scholar, Joel R. Soza, even suggests that the concept of a bachelor is so incomprehensible that there exists no word in the Hebrew language to describe it. The idea is that Jeremiah doesn't just carry news of Israel's tragedy, he not only occupies that place, but he actually embodies the undoneness of it all. Something laden with potential, now barren.

Jeremiah 31 is a common reading in the Christmas season. The familiarity of the passage might mean we miss the force of its words, and that this message of a new hope passed through chapped lips. Sometimes, those of us on this side of history merely nod at parts of the old stories with which we'd do better to sit. That's part of the waiting period, of Advent.

This is the prophet who inhabits an unfaithful land, who delivers God's harshest judgments, who feels them, and who endures long enough to say these words:

> "'The days are coming,' declares the Lord,
>   'when I will make a new covenant
> with the people of Israel.'" (Jer. 31:31)

Jeremiah tells a shattered people that, one day, God will again draw near. And this time, his ways will be written on hearts and he will be known beyond instruction. He will forgive and will establish a new covenant, one freed from the actions and inactions of men, one that begins a return to peace and fruitfulness, to Eden. Though dim still, it brightens. ■

REFLECT

Reflect on a time in your life when you felt caught in a cycle of unfaithfulness or broken commitments, either with God or with others. How did you experience God's conviction during that time?

Jeremiah's prophecy ultimately points to the coming of Jesus Christ, who establishes a new and eternal covenant through his sacrifice. How does knowing this shape your perspective on the significance of Christmas and the Advent season?

WHEN YOU'RE READY FOR JESUS TO RETURN

The weariness of trial
reveals our priorities.

BY KAREN STILLER

THERE WAS A MOMENT, in the aftermath of my husband's premature death, when I thought about Jesus coming back and longed for his return with an urgency I had never before experienced. I always knew we were supposed to long for the return of our king—a kind of obligation of anticipation. But I confess I had previously liked my life too much.

But now, I wanted him to stop all the delays. I imagined the moment arriving and seeing Jesus and thinking, "Yes, yes, there you are. Fantastic!" And then pushing past him as quickly as politely possible to search for my husband. (Is this what it will be like? A busy airport arrival lounge?)

I imagined throwing myself into his arms once again. (Dear God, please let it be a little bit like that.) I have never known such longing. And I know that this reveals my longings to be out of order. Of course they are. I feel a bit badly about this, but I can confess it to the God who knows us, and who I have discovered made us more resilient than we know and capable of so much love that the vastness of this love's loss causes grief to feel like an ocean.

Advent isn't normally about feeling badly about ourselves or our lives. That's Lent's job—the party pooper of the Christian liturgical year. Advent is more like that event planner friend who is cooking up a great feast and making all kinds of fantastic plans for the next month. We wait. We mark off days on the calendar. We are impatient as we prepare.

Enter Haggai. His name even means "festival," so he's perfect for Advent. He's also just what the returned exiles of 520 B.C. needed to get them moving on their temple rebuilding project, which they had been neglecting. The temple had fallen into disrepair during their forced absence. There was government pressure to leave the temple in ruins, and the people had been focusing their efforts on their own houses rather than the work of rebuilding God's house.

Haggai hears the call to speak into the lives of God's people. He stirs himself for the task and stirs the pot, prophetically speaking. He urges the people into action. They come to see their priorities have been misaligned and their longings have been in the wrong order. They find their courage. They start to rebuild and repair the temple.

"Work, for I am with you," says the Lord (2:4).

I wonder if there's a moment in the life of a prophet like Haggai, when they see that the message God gave them to deliver has both landed—hit the mark almost exactly—and they experience a moment of pleasure. A job well done. That is a fine thing to consider.

The sun came up for Haggai and his work crew, and it comes up now for us, each day as the morning turns to afternoon and we turn to work and toil. We sweep. We tidy. We build new temples and patch up the old ones. There is garbage to be taken out and fresh flowers to be put in vases. There is holiness to be seen to, and lived out of and toward, as much as we can muster, while we wait.

And what about our hearts that long? They can also be an offering. Our longings will all be swept up in joy that might feel even more vast than the ocean that grief becomes. We believe, and we wait.

We are in the afternoon of the most promising of days. So much more is to come. "I will shake all nations, and what is desired by all nations will come, and I will fill this house with glory," says the Lord Almighty (2:7). Come, Lord Jesus. Come. ∎

REFLECT

How does knowing that God is with you in your daily tasks and challenges impact your perspective on work?

Haggai's message to rebuild the temple speaks to aligning priorities with God's kingdom. In what ways do you find yourself prioritizing temporal concerns over spiritual investments?

ZECHARIAH'S FURNACE OF TRANSFORMATION

What silence and
solitude do to the soul.

BY CHRISTINA GONZALEZ HO

T IS TEMPTING to dismiss Zechariah as a fool for doubting Gabriel. After all, if a visitation from an archangel is possible, why not a miraculous pregnancy? Surely Zechariah, being a priest, knew the story of Abraham and Sarah, who also bore a son in their old age. But we know that logic can become puny in the face of deep disappointment or pain—and in Zechariah's case, the pain ran decades deep.

"Your prayer has been heard," the angel told him—a prayer he surely quit long ago, when the last hope for children disappeared with Elizabeth's fertility (Luke 1:13). After that, Zechariah must have resigned himself to his reality: He was childless, and always would be. That an angel had just blasted through the roof of that reality did not dispel it completely. After so many years of heartache, Zechariah had trouble believing.

Some time ago, my husband and I experienced a miscarriage. When we became pregnant again a few months later, I struggled with dread every day. Every time I felt a twinge, I was terrified it was a harbinger of something worse—stabbing pain, a gush of blood, unstoppable, irreversible loss. I found it difficult, almost impossible, to believe I was actually going to have a baby. One afternoon, as I sat on the couch, battered by wave upon wave of anxiety, I asked God for a clear sign the pregnancy would be successful. If this baby will be born healthy, let someone knock on our door right now. But even as I prayed, I knew no sign could take away my anxiety. The experience of loss was still too keen. If I'd seen an actual angel—who knows? But I've never waited for anything as long as Zechariah had.

To Zechariah, Gabriel said, "And now you will be silent and not able to speak until the day this happens, because you did not believe my words" (v. 20). Later, we are told Zechariah was struck deaf as well (v. 62). This sounds like a punishment. To be rendered suddenly without hearing or speech is to be isolated from others, forced into solitude—as Henri Nouwen writes in *The Way of the Heart*, "Silence completes and intensifies solitude." Yet Scripture does not present solitude and silence as punishments, but as invitations.

Solitude, writes Nouwen, is "the furnace of transformation." In the silence, stripped of worldly props and scaffolds, we are forced to confront our own "frightening nothingness." It is this excruciating vulnerability that becomes the doorway to God's presence, to the place where we surrender to his love. This is the solitude that Zechariah, through silence, was compelled to enter—the solitude of Moses' 40 years in the desert, and of Jesus' temptation in the wilderness.

With no distraction from his doubt—and no way to voice it, either—all that was left for Zechariah to do was listen. In the silence, God spoke to him again, and this time, he believed. When Zechariah finally spoke months later, it was to prophesy about the Messiah, in a song bursting with wonder, faith, and love. In the silence, Zechariah was transformed from a man of resignation to a man full of hope.

Silence, waiting, the relinquishing of control—these are painful experiences before they are life-giving ones. But the promise of the gospel is that someday life will come. Until then, we wait—like Zechariah, like Elizabeth—for the promises of God to be made manifest. Help us, Lord, to surrender to you in the silence and waiting, so that we too may be transformed. ■

REFLECT

Consider the role of silence and solitude in your spiritual life. How can periods of silence become opportunities for transformation and deeper intimacy with God?

Consider how Zechariah's story illustrates the painful yet life-giving process of relinquishing control. How can you practice surrender in your daily life?

HOW INSECURITY THWARTS A KINGDOM

Herod's violence reveals
the futility of earthly power.

BY RYAN KEATING

I T WAS A GROUP of astrologers "from the east" who first informed Herod that an heir to the Jewish throne had been born in his territory (v. 1). They must have traveled a long way, and I wonder if they had any idea what kind of man this king was. I imagine Herod making his visitors wait outside in the sun while he finished his lunch. And when he finally listened to their account of an auspicious star pointing to a royal birth, the significance of the story was difficult for him to digest.

Matthew tells us that "all Jerusalem" felt the upheaval in Herod's soul, where insecurity and contempt burned through stability and reason (v. 3). The deadly pistons of conspiracy churned, fueled by a reservoir of fear that he wouldn't have been able to acknowledge; but it must have escaped like steam from his expression and tone, obvious to anyone in his orbit.

He received the news of God's chosen deliverer as a threat. The existence of a tiny, legitimate, messianic king of Israel felt like an assault on the identity that Herod had constructed for himself, a brittle tower of power and self-importance. And the urgency of his arrogance and fragility was the only justification for wielding the coercive violence of the state to kill babies in broad daylight.

The Magi refused to participate in his plot. They were wiser men than Herod realized, which isn't surprising. His kind of pride and hatred make it difficult to truly see others for who they are; all of his internal energy was expended on convincing the world that he was as great as he imagined he should be.

After their visit with Jesus, the Magi escaped back to their country. It is scandalous and wonderful that these foreigners were the first to worship Jesus in Matthew's account. Although sometimes in subtle and subversive ways, Matthew highlights the radical inclusion of the nations in the new people of God throughout his gospel. In fact, many of my friends from places like Iran, Azerbaijan, and Kazakhstan all want to claim the Magi as having come from their homeland.

Matthew's version of the events also reveals a parallel with the Old Testament Exodus story. Like Herod, Pharoah had ordered the slaughter of babies in a desperate attempt to eliminate a perceived threat to power. The shrewdness of Shiphrah and Puah, wise midwives whose names are worth remembering, thwarted his evil plan (Ex. 1:15–21). And Moses, God's chosen deliverer, was rescued and raised in exile, which was, of course, God's plan all along.

I live as an exile on the island of Cyprus. I was unjustly deported from my former home by a leader who considers me a threat to national security. He doesn't want the good news of God's deliverance to spread. He cannot see the wisdom of our work caring for refugees. And he cannot see the goodness of the people we serve. But, now seven years later, I can see the hand of God moving us to complete a greater plan. And I am learning to focus on its goodness, and on his goodness, even when I am called to dark government offices to respond to false accusations in our new home as well. His kingdom is coming.

I imagine that Joseph and Mary were too inspired by the greatness of their son to let their lives be defined by bitterness toward Herod and the dark politics of the world around them. There were days to redeem and long afternoons to join in the work of hoping for the renewal of all things, even as they made the long walk back from Egypt and watched Jesus suffer alienation, false accusations, and persecution. In the end, after our own long days of waiting, we all join the Magi in worship. ■

REFLECT

Consider the contrast between the responses of Herod and the Magi to the news of Jesus. In what ways can you relate to either character in your own life?

Have you ever experienced persecution, felt marginalized, or been unjustly treated because of your faith or beliefs? How did you respond to those challenges?

ON THE HEELS
OF THE
MIRACULOUS

Joseph's call to obedience
in the midst of the mundane.

BY COURTNEY MOODY

SWEAT DRIPS off Joseph's forehead onto the dust road. The afternoon sun glares off his back and onto the sandy landscape. A pebble has lodged itself in his sandal. He'd love to stop and take it out before a blister forms, but there are miles to go, and Mary has finally calmed a now two-year-old Jesus back to sleep after their donkey was spooked by a snake.

Not too long ago, life had seemed wonderful beyond their wildest dreams. They'd been blessed with rich gifts from several wise men who followed God's star all the way from the East to see Jesus. The Messiah was here. Mary and Joseph had been specially chosen by God. It would be easy to assume Jesus would remember his earthly parents when the time came for him to overthrow the government and establish a new kingdom.

Then the warning came in the form of another dream. Despite doing his best to obey and explain to Mary their sudden need to flee the safety of their hometown, Joseph must have had questions rising within him with each step they took toward Egypt. What happened to the miracle? If Herod was threatening God's Son, why didn't God just strike him down? What were they to even make of all these dreams and angelic appearances?

I always find myself encouraged at this time of year—not just by the Nativity but by the many surrounding days that compose the season of Advent. Faith is easy when we're in the middle of a breakthrough: that amazing job offer, a miraculous doctor's report, the divine provision. But when life returns to the mundane, faith can become a challenge. Staying joyful as we go back to our jobs, washing dishes and clothes, and the many other tasks that clutter our lives, becomes the true test of faith. This is especially true when real, severe trial comes on the heels of the miraculous.

Attacks often come right after a spiritual high and place us on our own road to Egypt, calling us to test our confidence in the Lord. A miracle comes and reminds us of God's wonderful presence—and then comes the plunge into difficulty and uncertainty. We find ourselves asking the same questions that would have likely come to Joseph: What happened? Why doesn't God just fix this? Have I really heard from God?

Questions are natural. They can lead us to deepen our faith. When we take our questions to God, he draws near with comfort and answers. As Joseph looked back at Mary, he saw Jesus: the promise of the angel who appeared to him. God's Word made flesh. Breathing. Fidgeting. Tangible proof that God did and would come through.

Through Joseph's obedience, God would bring the family to safety in Egypt. Word would eventually reach them of what had occurred back in Bethlehem and turn into a testimony of divine intervention. As they remained there, Jesus would grow older. Immanuel would be with them, reminding them of the eternal presence of God and his promises. Waking up and sitting down to their morning meal with Jesus would be their reminder of God's faithfulness, and eventually, they would come out of Egypt and fulfill the prophecy of Hosea.

As we find ourselves underneath the beating sun of suffering or trial, wondering what happened to the miracles, we may find ourselves struggling even in our obedience. Perhaps our questions feel like a swirling sandstorm obscuring the guidance of God.

But just as Joseph could look to the Son of God for encouragement, so can we. In the fulfilled promises of Advent, we find comfort. Though the road to our own Egypt may seem long and filled with sweat and stones, Jesus is Immanuel, "God with us." In obedience, we can keep walking with our eyes on him, knowing that the cool breezes of the evening will eventually come and that the miracles have just begun. ∎

REFLECT

Consider Joseph's obedience to God's call to flee to Egypt. What challenges or doubts might he have faced during this journey?

Reflect on a time when you experienced a spiritual high followed by a trial or challenge. How did you navigate through it? What did you learn about your faith in those moments?

Recall and reflect on the stories of trial in this week's devotions. Imagine yourself in those scenarios.

What lessons about faithfulness, endurance, and trust in God's plan can you draw from their stories to navigate through your own trials and difficulties? What steps can you take this week to strengthen your faith in God's sovereignty amid trials?

Whose story did you most resonate with?

DAY 1 Jeremiah

DAY 2 Haggai

DAY 3 Zechariah

DAY 4 Herod

DAY 5 Joseph

Why?

W3

A TIME FOR
REVELATION

"For with you is the
fountain of life;
in your light we see light."

PSALM 36:9

THE
FUTURE'S
GREAT LIGHT

How Isaiah prophesies
the expectation of Advent.

BY MORGAN MITCHELL

AFTER THE HOURS of heat, the early evening beckons with a soft light and its pleasant coolness. The late hours crack the egg of the day to reveal the golden yolk of the setting sun. It would be a mind-bending exercise to try to explain darkness without describing light—it's likely impossible to do so. Light beckons on the horizon of even the darkest moments.

The prophet Isaiah, however, had awakened with the dawn. He was a prophet of Judah who ministered during the reign of four kings; the progeny of a family of rank and status; a family man; one who had a willing spirit to do what the Lord had called him to do. Commissioned to be a mouthpiece of God, he spoke with prophetic force even though his words would fall on deaf ears, and his throat would grow scratchy.

His work and writing bears some of the most profound words in all of Scripture, echoing themes of holiness, justice, allegiance, trust, righteousness, and hope. The words read today in Isaiah 9:2-7 reveal sparks of this truth, reflecting the contrast between light and dark, hope and heaviness, honor and gloom.

This contrast is foreshadowed even in the names that Isaiah gives his sons: the first named Shear-Jashub, or, "a remnant will return" and the second named Maher-Shalal-Hash-Baz as a warning, "quick to the plunder, swift to the spoil," a balancing act that neither contradict nor cancel each other out, but fleshes out the theme that this unified story directs us toward throughout the Advent season (7:3, 8:1).

We simply cannot explain the darkness without describing the light. "The people walking in darkness have seen a great light; on those living in the land of deep darkness a light has dawned" (v. 2).

When we turn away from God, there is a spiritual darkness that will haunt and startle us. After an amazing work of God in our hearts we begin to redirect, reroute, reorient ourselves toward light, and find it so real, so sustaining, that the noble crew of C. S. Lewis's Dawn Treader called it "drinkable". We begin to experience the goodness of things to come like "drinkable light" and that break in the clouds and sunlight on our back fuels the drumbeat to freedom—a freedom that comes from aligning our values, allegiance, obedience, delight, and hope with our God of unfailing love.

Isaiah knew that Bethlehem would be the place that God would hem the garments of eternity. This "Prince of Peace" would one day be acquainted with the truest form of darkness imaginable—a darkness no one else could endure—so that we may walk in the light.

Isaiah foresaw a future light and was welcoming the dawn that would one day break after a long, dark night, casting beams of hope 700 years into the future. He saw a radiant heir that would come as a peasant even as he was the Messiah. Jesus shines a light past the evening, awakens the dawn, and sets the course for redemptive history—a baby growing to be a man who would experience true darkness, so that we, with sleepy eyes, may gaze upon eternal light. ■

REFLECT

Isaiah prophesied about a future light that would dawn upon those walking in darkness. How does the imagery of light breaking into darkness resonate with your own journey of faith and life experiences?

Jesus is described as the "Wonderful Counselor, Mighty God, Everlasting Father, Prince of Peace." How do these names impact your view of who Jesus is in your life?

THE FRUIT AND FIRE OF THE SPIRIT

Mary's encounter with God's power
reveals the arc of the Spirit's work.

BY ALYSSA STADTLANDER

IMAGINE MARY, rubbing her eyes in the light cast by the angel in the doorway, the phosphorescence filtering through the dusty, dusky air of her room.

Some days, I imagine the angel appears to her as a young boy about her age, gazing at her with wide, curious eyes and cocked head, grinning as he makes his pronouncement about the good news that is coming through her. Other times, I imagine the angel as an older grandmother, kneeling in front of her and brushing the hair from her eyes, comforting her like a mother would upon delivering news that is about to change everything. Still other times, the angel is simply a flash of light, a pillar of fire in the wilderness, while Mary blinks, trying to absorb the message flooding her room, knowing that every moment in her life will arrange itself according to this one; there will be a before, and an after. "How shall this be?" Mary asks (v. 34, KJV throughout).

As an answer, the miraculous words from the angel slip into the warm air: "The Holy Ghost shall come upon thee, and the power of the Highest shall overshadow thee: therefore also that holy thing which shall be born of thee shall be called the Son of God. . . . For with God nothing shall be impossible" (vv. 35, 37).

And suddenly, something happens, full of life and earthy glory, the presence of God somehow forming that which is new and real inside Mary's womb.

The first time I heard these words—really heard them—I wept. Desperate to feel anything from El

Roi, the God who Sees, I longed for a glimpse of the Holy Spirit coming upon me, the arms of the Most High cradling my small body curled up on my college apartment couch. I envisioned my own light-filled hope that God indeed saw me and instilled purpose within me, that I was worth the effort of drawing near.

Isn't this what God is always doing, cultivating new mercies from a generous fount, an overshadow of his Spirit and a word of change? The poem of creation itself begins with these lines, a foreshadow of the kingdom to come:

> "And the earth was without form, and void; and darkness was upon the face of the deep. And the Spirit of God moved upon the face of the waters. And God said, Let there be light: and there was light" (Gen. 1:2–3).

This simple, impossible declaration that calls light out of darkness persists, enacted by a Spirit who is, even now, moving on our behalf. The same Spirit who lit the first sky with light, who became a pillar of fire in the wilderness, who poured out an unshakable presence into prophets, priests, and kings.

The same Spirit who overshadowed a young girl in Nazareth and created a holy thing inside her womb; the same Spirit who raised the girl's son, the Word of God made flesh, to life 30 years later; who flung tongues of fire upon humanity to light our way, that we might all—Gentile and Jew, slave and free, male and female—see the beauty and presence of God together. The same Spirit is living within you, too.

In the midst of our own uncertainties, as we face the coming night, our bodies—like Mary's, like Jesus'—have the capacity to hold the power of the Most High who is, even now, hovering over the face of the deep waters within us, creating a new way forward in the places we have deemed impossible.

This Advent season, may we practice echoing Mary's words of acceptance-"be it unto me according to thy word" (Luke 1:38)–and pay generous attention as the Spirit fills us with power and love. May we pause and wonder on the stoop of our soul as the sun sets, as we wait for the promised light. May we feel the pillar of fire within us burn. ■

REFLECT

Mary responds to Gabriel with faith and surrender, saying, "Let it be to me according to your word." How can Mary's response inspire you in moments of uncertainty or when facing unexpected challenges in your own life?

How can Mary's encounter with the angel prepare your heart to welcome Jesus anew into your life? What practices can you adopt during Advent to cultivate a sense of expectation and readiness for Christ's coming?

RESTLESS NIGHTS AND RENEWED CALLINGS

Clarity comes from God in the
midst of Joseph's anxious wrestling.

BY GEORGE SWEETMAN

THE GENEALOGY at the end of Matthew chapter 1 is curious, isn't it? After a long and, to many ears, boring list of begetting names and family lineages, the story ends with the news of Mary's scandalous pregnancy and Joseph grappling with a miserable decision—publicly shame Mary (with the resulting possibility of her death!) or divorce her without a fuss, but likely to a life of misery and loneliness.

There are nights that I fall into my pillows with a mind full of restless and toxic thoughts that keep me staring at my white ceiling and from much-needed sleep. Nonetheless, what occupies my mind is nothing compared to what Joseph was dealing with upon the news that Mary was pregnant. His days must have been filled with a paralyzing sadness at this betrayal, and nights restless with their tossing and turning as he faced what seemed like only two options. Imagine: You're excited about the prospects of marriage, you're moving through the betrothal stage of the process— more than an engagement but not yet marriage— working diligently to ensure that all is lined up for a wedding feast that will include friends, family, and days of eating, drinking, and celebrating only to be told months before the big day(s) that you're going to be a dad and, oh, by the way, the baby isn't yours (of course!) or even another man's!

When Joseph is finally able to sleep after stewing over the pain of his impending Solomonic decision, he is visited in his slumber, and the dream changes his life. A messenger from God appears to him and whispers, "Joseph son of David, do not be afraid to take Mary home as your wife, because what is conceived in her is from the Holy Spirit. She will give birth to a son, and you are to give him the name Jesus, because he will save his people from their sins" (Matt. 1:20–21).

Here's the thing: Joseph is a simple worker of wood; he is not any rabbi's apprentice. Nonetheless, he is a faithful Jew—going to temple on High Holy Days, observing feasts and fasts, and having some understanding of the Hebrew Scripture from the training of his youth. The angel's proclamation of the Spirit's presence could possibly have made some sense to him. And yet, what he's told in the depth of his REM sleep that night causes him to take massive action and redirect the entire course of his life. When Joseph wakes, he knows what to do. Does doubt linger? How could it not? Is he still confused? Probably. Does he begin to calculate the reputational cost of his obedience? Likely. But there is no wavering for Joseph.

The Spirit's work—that which began at the creation of the cosmos, continued through the kings and prophets as told in the early scrolls, and that animates his ancient world—that work must continue. It must be birthed. And the child, "Jesus"—not a unique name of that generation or time, but one with the immeasurably important promise *he will save his people from their sins*—will be received and cared for by his earthly father and presented to the world.

After nights struggling under a shroud of doom obscuring his family's future, Joseph rises that morning with a renewed call and a God-word that rests upon his shoulders. The dawn of a new day has begun. The dawn of a new life is promised. The dawn of a new creation is about to break through, and the dark of the night has been dispelled. Everything has been changed. ■

REFLECT

Consider the metaphor of dawn breaking after a night of struggle and uncertainty. How have you experienced God's faithfulness bringing new beginnings or fresh perspectives after seasons of darkness or difficulty?

Joseph's obedience to God's message changed the course of his life completely. Can you think of a time when your obedience to God's direction or calling resulted in significant life changes or a shift in your priorities?

THE ETERNAL TESTIMONY OF JESUS' PARENTS

Mary and Joseph's journey
to the tender heart of parenthood.

BY CALEB SAENZ

I CAN STILL REMEMBER our first trip home as a family after my daughter was born. I don't know that I had ever driven as safely or as slowly as I did when we left the hospital. We had been anticipating this moment for nearly a year, but for all the appointments and books and classes and redecorating, nothing prepared me for the sudden and colossal change I had undergone. I was now a father. The safety net of the hospital was disappearing in the rearview mirror, and each creaking mile took me further into an entirely new reality.

The complicated thing about parenting is that you receive an identity change before you really know what to do with it. I became a father when I first heard my daughter cry. She's ten now, and in so many ways I am still becoming her father. What might have felt akin to impostor syndrome early on has shifted into an indelible piece of who I am. Faithfulness through success and failure has yielded the fruit of that change.

I think about this experience often when I read about Joseph. Matthew describes him as a righteous man, who prioritized care for his betrothed and obedience to the law of Moses. When he sees that Mary is pregnant, before they were married and could conceive, his response indicates that he holds his righteousness even above his heartache, as he likely suspects infidelity. But as he moves toward a quiet divorce, saving Mary public shame, a messenger of God intervenes as Joseph is dreaming one night. The child in Mary's womb is the work of the Holy Spirit, he is told, and this son will save God's people from their sins. The dream ends, and Joseph rises to a new identity and with it, a new world. He might have gone to bed a heartbroken man, but he wakes up a committed husband and father.

Mary's experience is the focal point of the other three gospel accounts, and they provide a vivid depiction of what it looks like for her to faithfully respond to the word of God. Our experience with the Holy Spirit operates on a similar trajectory. We are forever changed by grace at the core of who we are, and the new life inside of us is to be displayed as a tangible testimony. We nurture and care for what is within so that it might go out to serve the world around us.

In Matthew's gospel, Joseph presents us with a different vantage point. While Mary nurtured life toward its external revelation, Joseph is called as a father to witness something outside of himself that will one day occupy the center of his heart.

After the message in his dream, Joseph's whole life became an expression of waiting. The promise from God's messenger carried no details or dates. Joseph is to be Jesus' earthly father, but his choice to receive that calling is less a one-time acceptance and more a daily choice to follow through with his new identity and the responsibilities it entails.

I will not attempt to speak for the Bible in its silence, but we know the realities of parenting that Joseph would have experienced. We can faithfully imagine his heart swelling as he heard Jesus' first words. We can picture Joseph hurting with Jesus, as the Son wept over his first cut or scrape. Joseph, righteous and obedient, called to fatherhood in a dream, was surely learning to be a father as he watched Jesus dream peacefully in his sleep. This humble man who followed behind a toddler clumsily racing through his home will one day follow proudly behind a triumphant, risen king.

Advent shows us there is a burden and a beauty after awakening. Those who have seen a great light carry a responsibility to steward new life. But what is within us is at work around us, too. All things are indeed being made new. Joseph teaches us that those who wait will also witness. ∎

REFLECT

Reflect on the idea of awakening to new responsibilities and callings. How does this concept resonate with your own experiences of spiritual growth and transformation?

Parenthood often involves embracing a new identity. How can Mary and Joseph's journey encourage you in your own role, regardless of the challenges you may face?

TO SEE A PROPHECY FULFILLED

Witnessing God's ways
through Simeon's eyes.

BY LILY JOURNEY

THE PROPHETIC VISIONS splintered through Simeon's mind in a fraction of a second as a teenage girl and young man walked up the temple steps with their child. The images of what had been and would come, contained within this bundle coming to meet him.

War and rumors of war.
Peace and a marriage feast.

A scrap of linen swaddling cloth.
Linen temple drapes torn in half.

The groans of a Jewish girl laboring in a stable.
The tear-stained cheeks of a mother kneeling at a cross.

Each image pointed to the completion of the promise he'd waited for his whole life: a Messiah who would usher in a world turned upside down on itself, a world where the meek were strong and the rich became poor. He might have laughed at the irony of the sight before him. A tiny baby with the strength to snuff out death, and an impoverished couple witnessing the greatest coronation in history. This is the blessing Simeon would give the God-child as his calloused hands held the infant: the blessing of paradox, for he will be the rise and fall of many Israelites.

Luke doesn't write much about Simeon beyond describing him as a "righteous and devout man" (v. 25). We aren't given the detailed story of the day Simeon met Jesus, and the gaps leave ripe room for imagining what Simeon experienced during those long-awaited moments. What did it feel like to wait all those years? Was he ever tempted to speed up the process, to look for the Savior another way?

As we peer through Simeon's ancient eyes, we realize that the promise of Advent is both slow and mysterious. It requires both waiting and wondering. Personally, I'm not very good at slowness. I tend to sprint through Advent with the rest of the world, dutifully ticking away the days on my December calendar; hurry through the mysterious and confusing bits; get to the candlelit "Silent Night" and festive presents. I rush though as if the less I think about the grit of Bethlehem, the more I can enjoy the twinkling lights and Christmas trees and gingerbread houses. My impatience is a way to resist the lingering questions.

But then I remember Simeon. Simeon waited. And waited. Along with many of the other prophets in the Bible, Simeon dwelled in the paradox of Advent for years. Unlike me with my chocolate calendar, Simeon didn't have the luxury of a countdown or the ease of knowing how the story would end. He just got comfortable with the one thing he knew: God would fulfill what he had promised.

We, like Simeon, are waiting in the afternoon shadows of the in-between between Jesus' saving work on the cross and the ultimate redemption of his second coming. The scandal of the Christmas story is that it flips our vision of the world upside down and gives us a new way of seeing. In doing so, it demands that we surrender our tendency to rush and to rationalize. How would the Christmas story change for us if we allowed ourselves to be wrapped up in the radical profundity of it all—of a child that causes both "falling and rising" (v.34)? Of divinity intermingled with the gritty, ordinary chaos of humanity? If we paused long enough, what pains, questions, and promises would bubble up to the surface? Advent offers us the gentle invitation to model Simeon's posture, waiting patiently, pondering, and wondering. ■

REFLECT

Like Simeon, how can you cultivate a posture of patient waiting and wonder in your own spiritual journey, especially during the Advent season?

Reflect on the "afternoon shadows of the in-between" described in the devotional. How do you experience the tension between the present realities of suffering and the future promise of redemption?

Recall and reflect on this week's stories of God's divine revelation of his presence in the lives of his beloved.

How can the experiences from this week's stories deepen your understanding of God's revelation of his presence and work in your life and community? What steps can you take this week to cultivate a deeper spiritual sensitivity in your daily life?

Whose story did you most resonate with?

DAY 1 Isaiah

DAY 2 Mary

DAY 3 Joseph

DAY 4 Mary + Joseph

DAY 5 Simeon

Why?

W 4

A TIME FOR

WONDER

"Sing to the Lord, all the earth; proclaim
his salvation day after day. Declare his
glory among the nations, his marvelous
deeds among all peoples."

PSALM 96:2-3

CHRISTMAS BECKONS US WITH WONDER

How the incarnation of Christmas
can change our perspective.

BY ISAAC GAY

Y IN-LAWS LIVE on three acres in western New York. A creek runs behind their house, holding the memories of my wife and her siblings playing in it as children. Their laughter is now echoed by the giggles of our children. Rows of evergreens line the property, enfolding the highs, lows, and nuances of family life. One winter's night, as I strolled through the snow piled on the path and in the branches, my mind drifted to a vision of the "age to come." As millions of snowflakes with their unique expression of God's creative genius fell around me, I was once again introduced to wonder.

The French word *inspirer*, the source of the English word *inspiration*, is literally translated as *breath*. In the pause between our breaths, we are once in a while brought to a place of inspiration where we can observe what was previously hidden to us; our eyes glimpse the new that will one day be revealed.

As we see through the eyes of children, inspiration and wonder are the original postures of the human soul—as Jesus says, "Truly, I say to you, whoever does not receive the kingdom of God like a child shall not enter it" (Mark 10:15, ESV). The poet Dylan Thomas put it this way: "Children in wonder watching the stars / Is the aim and the end." As mature, regulated adults, we often find ourselves neglecting everyday wonder and conserving it as a response most appropriate to the monumental and palatial. We compartmentalize our day-to-day living and can easily lose the sense of humble availability that allows children to engage with the world around them in wonder. If we're not careful, our pride, pragmatism, and self-dependence can strip us of the essence that makes us most human, causing us to shut our eyes to the wonder that children see so easily.

The story of God's incarnation invites a childlike posture of wonder. Amid presuppositions of a kingly birth, Christ is born into unremarkable circumstances. Much like those who awaited the Messiah at the time, our modern eyes would have overlooked Bethlehem in favor of Jerusalem. We would have ignored the shepherds on the hillside as we do beggars on the streets, looking instead for the expected grandeur of glory. But when we come to the scene of the baby lying in the manger, we find the epitome of wonder. Redirecting our gaze back to the humble and wonderful, God meets humanity in the most mundane of ways. The Incarnation reminds us that as we pause, our ability to stand in wonder is no longer predicated on magnitude, but is available in monotony.

As we gather with our loved ones and enter into the season of lights and holly, sleigh bells and nativity, it is good to gaze at the elementary; to stand in wonder during a snowfall, to delight in the taste of freshly baked pastries, to laugh along to the sound of children playing, and to answer the door to childlike faith that wonder can open. Not only do we find Christ there, but we find him inviting us to share in the way he sees the world he has created. ■

REFLECT

Reflect on a moment in your life when you experienced a profound sense of wonder or awe. What was happening around you, and how did that experience deepen your appreciation for God's beauty and power?

The devotional mentions the importance of receiving the kingdom of God like a child. How can you cultivate a childlike posture of wonder in your own life, especially during the Advent season?

A PROMISE
IN THE
DARKNESS

What Isaiah's prophecy means
for us during dark nights.

BY KIMBERLY PHINNEY

Y DAUGHTER is afraid of the dark. So, as a rational adult who's supposed to know there is nothing to fear when we switch off the lights, I try to abate her cries with reason. But no matter what I say, it doesn't work. The only remedy that brings her peace is the assurance of my presence: "Don't worry, I'm here with you." So, as I settle in beside her and await her heavy breaths of slumber, I wonder what it is about the pitch of night that is so unnerving—not just for our children but for all of us.

Mankind has feared the dark in its various forms since time began, as made clear in our ancestors' fireside epics and the torrid arc of history. I, too, came to fear this darkness in the grip of a chronic illness, which nearly took my life in 2021, as sepsis raged through my frail body after a failed surgery. So, perhaps our children's fear of the dark isn't without merit; rather, it is the first pang of the dread we adults have come to know as the very real anxieties that keep us up at night.

Children's darkened rooms serve as a foretaste of evil they know little about, as shadows of their once familiar toys become harbingers of ruin. The day this imaginative void becomes something true is the day our children learn, like those of us who have gone before them, that there really is a flip side to the coin of life: good and evil, peace and war, health and sickness, life and death.

Isaiah, the messianic prophet of the Bible, knew about this darkness, but despite the black cloak of chaos and war that surrounded him, he anticipated a far greater flip side: a coming Light—with a capital "L"—because this Light would arrive as a baby and forever redeem the dark side of the coin. Isaiah prophesied, "For to us a child is born, to us a son is given . . . and he will be called Wonderful Counselor, Mighty God, Everlasting Father, Prince of Peace" (Isa. 9:6). This Light would bring justice, righteousness, and peace with "no end" (v. 7). Isaiah urges the people of God to take heart! I can almost hear him now, speaking into my own darkness and its aftermath: *Dear soul, hold on! Hope for your suffering and light for your darkness are here! The Messiah is coming, and he will reign for eternity!*

Light is referenced in the Bible more than 250 times, and each time its symbolism is clear: Light represents the presence of God, Christ, and holiness. In his 2013 Advent sermon, the late Dr. Timothy Keller calls Isaiah's prophecy of Christ "the unexpected, ultimate Light." Christ is the Light that "came to overcome the deep darkness of the world," Keller exhorts. Thus, Christmas is the birth of Light—the great panacea for all that plagues mankind in the shadows. This is why the Advent season brings with it great anticipation and is a time so many look forward to. But there is a "withness" in Isaiah's prophecy that is for us all year round, in whatever darkness or suffering we face.

I asked my daughter what it is about my presence that helps her overcome her fear of the dark, and she said, "It solves my loneliness." We might not be so different from our children after all. If we face the darkness alone, there is reason for great fear. But if we believe in Christ's "withness"—his promise, *I am here with you*—then we, too, can find a reason to breathe our own deep sighs of relief in the darkness, so that we might sleep to dream and then to anticipate the greatest coming Light of all. Alone in my hospital bed, I learned this hard and beautiful truth firsthand: We must endure great darkness in this world, but we also know the bearer of all light. For it is written in John 1:4–5, "In him was life, and that life was the light of all mankind. The light shines in the darkness, and the darkness has not overcome it." ■

REFLECT

Isaiah prophesied about a coming Light, Jesus Christ, who would bring justice, righteousness, and peace. How does Jesus fulfill these promises in your life or in the world around you?

Reflect on a time when you or someone you know experienced fear or anxiety, whether in the literal or metaphorical darkness in life. How did God's presence bring peace in that situation?

AWAY IN A MANGER, HUMILIATED

The great conundrum of
weakness and power.

BY VIJAY KRISHNAN

IF YOU'VE EVER HAD the enjoyable (and chaotic) experience of being involved in a children's Christmas play, you probably remember the scene at the inn. Perhaps you were cast as the stern innkeeper whose first-century version of a Motel 6 was full for the night. Eventually, his reluctant generosity overtakes him and he makes space for the young couple out back with the animals. Or perhaps you were cast as a sheep. ("There are no small parts," they said.)

It's almost a throwaway verse for Luke, helping to explain why the Savior of the world ended up in a feeding trough for his first night on the planet. But attentive readers of Luke's entire gospel will see that he takes great care throughout his narrative to highlight the state of contrasts (rich vs. poor; proud vs. humble) that surround Jesus, and in particular the contrasting responses to Jesus. Luke 2:7, then, is no throwaway.

Not only does it highlight the incredible humiliation that Jesus and his family endured (and which Jesus continued to choose throughout his life and ministry), but it hints at something else—something that would also be a continued theme throughout Jesus' life: Rejection.

Consider that Joseph and Mary were returning to their hometown, Bethlehem, where there no doubt would have been extended family still residing, and many more returning for the census. It would have been customary (if not an absolute given) for Mary and Joseph to be invited to stay with relatives. Most houses had guest rooms of some kind, for situations just like this. For context, Luke uses the word translated "inn" in the story of the Good Samaritan in Luke 10:34 when referring to an actual commercial inn, whereas the translation here seems to refer more closely to a guest room. Are we to assume that all the guest rooms in every home of any relative of Joseph's were full? Wouldn't priority have been given to a very pregnant relative?

The answer would have likely been "yes," unless there was a stigma associated with this pregnancy. Unless Mary and Joseph arrived in his hometown under the whispers and cut-eye of a shameful situation.

The fact that the Son of God was born in a cave set aside for animals instead of a warm, safe, and much more sanitary guest room, surrounded by a doting and loving family, is not simply a product of a busy night on the motel strip. We should read this as another prophetic foreshadowing of just how difficult life was going to be for Jesus and his parents. The stigma, shame, and resulting rejection by extended family and friends made clear in this manger scene is a recurring theme in the Gospels.

The manger represents not only the humility of Jesus but also his humiliation. The manger in which he was laid is as much a symbol of rejection as is the cross on which he died. It tells us that from the beginning to the end, our Savior's life was marked, scarred, and difficult.

And yet, we cannot miss what immediately follows verse 7 in Luke's account: At the same time that he was being shamed and rejected by the ones he came to save, all the hosts of heaven were declaring his honor, his glory and his reign. Indeed, the shepherds who also felt a sense of rejection and ignominy would come running to see and worship him, caught up in the great mystery, the great conundrum of humiliation and glory; of weakness and power. ■

REFLECT

Think about the stigma and shame that Joseph and Mary might have faced in Bethlehem. How do you react to situations where you or others face societal judgment?

Consider the juxtaposition of Jesus' rejection by humans and his honor declared by heavenly hosts. What can we learn from this reality?

GLORY IN THE EYES OF THE SHEPHERDS

How angelic wonder initiates
the announcement of Christmas.

BY JULIA BARTEL

DO NOT BE AFRAID." Each time an angel appears in Luke's nativity story, they say these words. Mary hears them from Gabriel during the Annunciation; Gabriel speaks them to Zechariah, too, when he appears in the temple (Luke 1:13, 30). Now, in the breaking dawn of Christmas, we hear them a third time as humble shepherds witness an inbreaking of supernatural wonder in the unlikeliest of places.

Angels represent God's power and glory whenever they appear in the biblical narrative. Their holiness is otherworldly to us; they may be the closest thing in the Bible to aliens. Their appearance in the world initiates an overlapping of heavenly reality with earthly life so powerful and extraordinary that it causes those who see it to fall on their faces in awe and fear. Luke 2 details the terror that the shepherds felt as "the glory of the Lord shone around them" (v. 9). They were utterly overwhelmed by the sight.

It seems odd that heavenly beings, messengers of the Lord in all their extraordinary glory, would rush to comfort those who are witnessing this power. Yet here, that is exactly what the angel does. "Do not be afraid," he tells them, and goes on to share the news of "great joy for all the people:" the Messiah has been born (vv. 9-10).

That God's heavenly messengers speak words of reassurance, as they often do throughout their biblical appearances, points to the character of God and to the way the supernatural world is ordered under him. In this moment in Luke 2, the angel's majestic glory points not to himself, but to the greater glory of the incarnate God; his words of consolation point to the Savior who, at that moment, had finally arrived to bring comfort to a hurting world. The moment of announcement to the shepherds juxtaposes the terrifying glory of the Lord with his loving purposes: using his power not to harm, but to comfort; not to scare, but to strike with wonder; altogether pointing to Jesus, in whom these seemingly diametric aspects of God's character are perfectly united.

As the shepherds heard the angel's words of comfort and joy, awestruck—perhaps doing their best to comfort their frightened sheep—they witnessed only a sliver of the full glory of the Good Shepherd, the Great Comforter, the Sacrificial Lamb whose blood would redeem the world. ∎

REFLECT

Consider how you respond to moments of divine intervention or unexpected blessing. How can you cultivate a sense of awe and gratitude in your daily life?

Think about a moment when you felt small or insignificant. How does this story of the shepherds speak to you about God's view of human worth?

CHRISTMAS
DAY

THE ULTIMATE
WONDER

Celebrating the dependence
and sacrifice of Christmas Day.

BY GABRIELLE
MCCULLOUGH

I'LL NEVER FORGET the first moment the nurses laid him on my chest. The sound of a cry that screamed of helplessness. His body shocked by cold air but warmed by the comfort of my skin. The way his lips opened and closed, rooting for his hunger to be satisfied. The way his eyes were looking for someone who was looking at him. It's in this kind of utter need that unconditional love is found. This love is what I find my days filled with in this season; both the joy and chaos of caring for a newborn baby boy, dependent on me in almost every way. He relies on me for nourishment, for comfort, for help in the big and small; he is physically and emotionally helpless without the care of his parents. It is now more than ever, on Christmas Day as I stare into the precious eyes of my baby son, that I am struck by the humility of our Savior who chose this state of vulnerability as his marvelous entrance into the world.

Luke 2:6–7 gives an account of this entrance, as "the time came for [Mary] to give birth. And she gave birth to her firstborn son and wrapped him in swaddling cloths and laid him in a manger, because there was no place for them in the inn" (ESV). There was no palace, no red carpet rolled out for Jesus Christ. The Savior of the world, the king who is enthroned forever, was born of the virgin Mary and likely placed in a feeding trough used for animals. Our almighty God willingly chose dependence and weakness. He was subject to the full mortality of man in order that he might live a sinless life, and die a sinner's death, to be our perfect substitute that we might be reconciled to the Father by grace through faith. It's the greatest story of love and most radical expression of sacrifice in all of history. God became flesh and dwelt among us (John 1:14) so that he might save us through his life, death, and resurrection.

Both in our current era, where leadership is equated with a big stage and a large following, and in the Roman Empire, where force and domination were the norm, Jesus' incarnation is the most countercultural form of leadership we can imagine. Where we are way too easily impressed by worldly markers of success, and search for significance in our own independence, Jesus' birth and embrace of utter dependence completely flips the script on how we ought to view influence. His leadership is service; he bends down low and draws near to us in gentleness; he forfeits his might to lay his life down, both through his entrance in a manger and his exit on the cross.

As followers of Jesus and the way of life he offers his creation, the Christmas season offers an invitation to meditate on the humility of Jesus and seek to follow his lead. May we trade a craving for power for a craving for sacrifice. May we be marked by our patience with those who hurt us, our service to the least of these, and our unconditional love for our neighbor. And as we follow in his way, may we also assume a posture under his care as weak, needy, and dependent, for we are completely helpless without him. On Christmas Day, Jesus became weak in human form so that we might find life through him and his ultimate power. ■

AN INVITATION
WRITTEN
IN THE STARS

The wonder and conviction
that lead us to the king.

BY KEN SHIGEMATSU

I N THE FILM *CONTACT*, there is an emotional scene where the astronomer Ellie Arroway, played by Jodie Foster, explains to her friend her decision to venture into outer space, despite the clear dangers. She says, "For as long as I can remember, I've been searching for something, some reason why we're here. What are we doing here? Who are we? If this is a chance to find out even just a little part of that answer . . . I don't know, I think it's worth a human life. Don't you?"

We may not have a yearning to venture into outer space, but at a conscious or unconscious level, we all want to know why we're here—we long to discover the meaning of our existence. Despite this innate human longing, we discover something surprising in another story with cosmic proportions. In the story of the Magi, it is revealed that we are not the greatest seekers—God is.

The Magi have been described across many centuries as the wise men. Were they wise? Yes, but not in the way we typically think of. They were experts in discerning the meaning of the stars.

A Jewish person would have regarded the Magi— magicians, astrologers, and sorcerers—as idolaters, as Gentiles who were racial, cultural, and spiritual outsiders in the family of the one true God.

So why does Matthew include these Gentiles in an account written primarily to Jews? It seems that Matthew wants to show us that God seeks outsiders and invites them to the birthday party of his Son.

No matter what our racial or cultural background, regardless of what we have or haven't done, or how we feel we've fallen short of our own standards or our Creator's—God also seeks us out.

In Matthew's account, we see that while the star leads the Magi to Jerusalem, it's Scripture that ultimately leads them to Jesus. When King Herod heard about the star that announced the birth of the great king, he gathered all the high priests and religious scholars and asked where the Messiah was to be born. "In Bethlehem," they answered. Then they quoted words of Scripture from Micah 5:

> But you, Bethlehem, in the land of Judah,
> are not the least among the rulers of Judah;
> for out of you shall come a ruler
> who will shepherd my people Israel. (Matt. 2:6)

The star got the Magi to the "target" of Jerusalem, but it was Scripture that took them to the "bull's-eye" of Bethlehem—to Jesus. God can use all kinds of things, including beauty and affliction, to draw us closer to Jesus, but the vehicle that God often uses to lead us most clearly to Jesus is Scripture.

However, simply being exposed to Scripture or knowing the Bible isn't enough. The chief priests and teachers of the law knew that a star had announced the birth of the great king and that this anointed ruler, the Messiah, would be born in Bethlehem, yet they did not make the brief six-mile journey there.

It's possible for us to be exposed to Scripture and yet not respond. Years later, Jesus would say to the religious elite, "You study the Scriptures diligently because you think that in them you have eternal life. These are the very Scriptures that testify about me, yet you refuse to come to me to have life" (John 5:39–40).

This Advent, as we allow the wonder of the stars and the conviction of Scripture to lead us afresh to Jesus, we can know great joy like the Magi of old. And also like the Magi, as we bow down in adoration before Jesus, we will find in him the true meaning of our lives. ∎

REFLECT

Consider the joy and adoration the Magi experienced when they found Jesus. How can you cultivate a similar sense of joy and worship in your own life as you draw near to Jesus during this Advent season?

The Magi were outsiders—Gentiles who were not part of the Jewish community. How does their inclusion in the story of Jesus' birth influence your perception of how God seeks and invites us into relationship with him?